iPad Air & iPad mini
Users Manual

The Beginner to Expert Guide with Tips & Tricks to Master your iPad Air/Mini & Troubleshoot Common Problems

Henry A. White

Copyright © 2019 by Henry A. White- All rights reserved.

No part of this publication **iPad Air & iPad Mini Users Manual** may be reproduced, stored in a retrieval system or transmitted in any form or by any means, electronic, mechanical, photocopying, recording, and scanning without permission in writing by the author.

Contents

Introduction 1

How to Set Up Your New iPad Air/iPad Mini 2

How To Set Up Mail, Contacts, And Calendars On iPad 10

    How To Set Up Outlook.Com Mail, Calendar, And Contacts On iPad 11

    Setting Up Exchange Mail, Calendar, And Contacts On iPad 12

    How To Set Up IMAP/POP, Caldav, And Carddav On iPad 13

How To Adjust Display Zoom On iPad 14

Customize The Dock 15

Swipe Up to Go Home 16

Access App Switcher 16

Quit Apps 17

Use Apps in Floating Windows 17

Use Split View for Multitasking 18

Drag and Drop Files or Text Between Apps 19

Watch Videos in Picture in Picture 19

New Way to Access Control Center 20

Quick Gesture For App Switching 20

Quickly Access Spotlight From Anywhere 21

Use Apple Pencil To Take Notes on Lock Screen 21

Close Multiple Tabs in Safari 22

Lock Notes 23

Use Screen Time to Monitor Time Spent 24

Set App Limits 25

Move Multiple Apps Together on Home screen 26

Use The Hidden Cursor Mode 27

Enable AssistiveTouch 27

Add Website To Home Screen 28

Use Shortcuts App For Automation 29

Record Your iPad Screen 30

How to Take a Screenshot 30

Add Multiple Fingers to Touch ID 30

Use The Smart Keyboard and Master The Keyboard Shortcuts ... 31

Turn off keyboard clicks 33

The Quickload bar 33

The notifications bar – how to use it 34

Dictation keyboard 34

How to change wallpapers 35

Turn off Push/fetch email 36

Switch off location services 36

Check out the Privacy menu to keep control 37

Alerts and notifications 37

Do Not Disturb 38

iii

How to Disable Apple Music Listening History On iPhone And iPad 38

Transfer Your Cellular Data Plan From Your Old iPad To Your New iPad.. 39

How to play your video files 40

Set a volume limit (good for kids) 41

iTunes Match... 41

How to play FLAC files on an iPad mini.. 42

iTunes U 43

How to use AirPrint.. 43

Apple Pay 44

    How to Manage Apple Pay 44

    How to Use Wallet 45

How To Set up 'Hey Siri' on iPad 45

    How to Train "Hey Siri" to Your Voice 46

    How to Use "Hey Siri!"... 47

    How Secure Is "Hey Siri!" Voice ID?... 48

How to use iCloud 49

Switch search engines... 50

How to delete apps 54

Inverted colors 54

Move multiple apps at once 56

Split View in Safari 58

iv

Type faster with Key Flicks 60

How to Crop or Zoom a Video on iMovie for iOS 62

The Virtual Touchpad 72

Open Apps and Find Music and Quickly Using Spotlight Search .. 74

Download Free Books on Your iPad 75

Move an App to the iPad's Dock 77

Let Your iPad Read Selected Text to You 79

Changes to Notifications in iOS 12 81

How to Hide Pictures From the Photos App in iOS 12 88

How to Use iCloud Keychain on Your iOS Devices 90

Troubleshooting common problems 95

Introduction

The new 2019 iPad Air bridges the gap between the standard iPad and the new iPad Pro. You get access to a laminated 10.5-inch display, A12 Bionic Chip and you get support for Smart Keyboard and first-generation Apple Pencil. The new iPad mini 5 breathes new life into a form factor that's four years old at this point. The iPad mini 5 is easily the best and most powerful small tablet you can buy.

This makes the new iPads great content consumption and creation machine. All the professional apps will still run on the iPad Air and iPad mini 5. Once you've bought the new iPad, you'll want to set it up just right. Let's get started!

How to Set Up Your New iPad Air/iPad Mini

1. *Slide to Start Setting up*

When you power on your new iPad, you will see the interface below and slide from left to right with your finger on the screen. Then, you are asked to select a language, and the country or region choices will come next so that you can make choices of them depending on yourselves.

2. *Wi-Fi Network and Location Services Setting*

You are required to select a Wi-Fi entry from the listed options and click "Join" with its password. When the location services screen is shown, tap "Enable Location Services" to position your new iDevice. If you do not want to apply these services, choose "Disable Location Services."

Note: Location Service owns apps to position your exact location, which is helpful to give you direction when you get lost. Moreover, it works with many apps to give you tips about situation surrounding, so it is worthy-recommended.

3. *Set up iPad*

There are three choices listed on the "Set Up iPad" screen. Different options have distinguished ways to set up your iPad.

- Set up A New iPad
- Restore from iTunes Backup
- Restore from iCloud Backup

Set up A New iPad

Select "Set Up as New iPad" if it is your first time to use iDevice. Then, you need to select "Create a Free Apple ID." Otherwise, you can directly choose "Sign in with Your Apple ID."

Tips: When creating a free Apple ID, you need to enter your birthday to avoid troubles without a password. According to the age, if necessary, a parent must create your Apple ID.

After signing in or creating your Apple ID and password, choose "Use iCloud" so that you can backup your iOS data and transfer files among iOS devices and computer, which only has 5G storage.

iCloud

Use iCloud

Don't Use iCloud

What is iCloud?

iCloud lets you access your music, photos, contacts, calendars, and more on all of your devices, automatically.

About iCloud

When the next screen as following comes to you, you'd better choose "Use Find My iPad" lest you can't get it back when it gets lost. Moreover, select the number and email address so that your friends can keep in touch with you by iMessage and Face Time.

Find My iPad

Find My iPad is automatically enabled when you use iCloud.
It allows you to locate, lock, and erase your iPad if you ever lose it.
In addition, your Apple ID password will be required before anyone can erase or reactivate your iPad.

You can manage or turn off Find My iPad in iCloud Settings.

About Find My iPad

iMessage and FaceTime

LET OTHER PEOPLE REACH YOU AT:

marcwebbc@icloud.com ✓

marcwebbc@outlook.com ✓

New outgoing messages, FaceTime, and FaceTime Audio calls will be sent from "marcwebbc@outlook.com." You can change this in Settings.

What are iMessage and FaceTime?

People can contact you on all your devices via iMessage and FaceTime using your phone number or email addresses.

You will be asked to make choices according to the interface below. Tap "Use Siri" which can help solve your questions and "Automatically Send" in Diagnostics screen as well as "Share with App Developers" on the next interface.

iPad Air & iPad Mini Users Guide　　　　　　　　　　　　Henry A. White

Notes: Diagnostics would send your iPad data to Apple and allow Apple to know more about your iPad to improve its products. At the same time, App Analytics shares data with Apple to improve the apps.

Congratulation! All setting is accomplished and what will come to you is "Welcome to iPad" screen.

Welcome to iPad

Get Started

Restore from iTunes Backup

If you owned an iDevice before or you just had updated your iOS, you could select "Restore from iTunes Backup." Thus, you must connect your iPad to PC to move on iTunes on a computer with clicking "Restore Backup" on the right side.

Restore from iCloud Backup

You may not always take USB cable with you, so you can choose "Restore from iCloud Backup," but you must connect with Wi-Fi and then choose certain backup files you tend to restore.

Note: If you haven't backed up data on iTunes/iCloud before, you could use the first option "Set Up as a New iPad," and then utilize iPhone Transfer to move the data from computer to New iPad Air/iPad Mini, including contacts, photos, etc.

It is really simple to set up your new iPad Mini/iPad Air. Only if you can move on step by step on the screen, then can your new iPad start to be used.

How To Set Up Mail, Contacts, And Calendars On iPad

No matter if you use iCloud, Gmail, or another email, calendar, or contact service, it's pretty easy to set up these on your iPad. While the old "Mail, Contacts, & Calendars" section of Settings is gone, having been split up into separate sections, there's still only one place you need to go to set up your email, contact, and calendar accounts. Here's how to setup email, contacts, and calendars on iPad.

If you're looking to set up an iCloud account on your iPad, you'll want to follow the steps here (follow these steps if you already have an Apple ID):

- Open **Settings**.
- Tap **Passwords & Accounts**.
- Tap **Add Account**.
- Tap **Google**.
- Enter your **Google account credentials**.
- Make sure the *switches* for mail, contacts, and calendars are in the 'on' or 'off' positions depending on where you want them.
- Tap *Save*.

How To Set Up Outlook.Com Mail, Calendar, And Contacts On iPad

- Open **Settings**.
- Tap **Passwords & Accounts.**

- Tap **Add Account.**
- Tap **Outlook.com**.
- Enter your **Outlook.com account credentials.**
- Tap **Yes**
- Make sure the *switches* for mail, contacts, and calendars are in the 'on' or 'off' positions depending on where you want them.
- Tap *Save*.

Setting Up Exchange Mail, Calendar, And Contacts On iPad

- Open **Settings**.
- Tap **Passwords & Accounts.**
- Tap **Add Account.**
- Tap *Exchange.*
- Enter your *Exchange email address.*
- Tap *Next*.
- Tap *Configure Manually.*
- Enter your *Exchange account information* if you elected to configure your

account manually (you might need to get these from your IT administrator if you don't know them).
- Tap *Next*.
- Make sure the *switches* for mail, contacts, and calendars are in the 'on' or 'off' positions depending on where you want them.
- Tap *Save*.

How To Set Up IMAP/POP, Caldav, And Carddav On iPad
- Open **Settings**.
- Tap **Passwords & Accounts**.
- Tap **Add Account.**
- Tap *Other*.
- Select the *type* of account you want to configure. Select Mail for an email account CalDAV for a calendar, and CardDAV for contacts.
- Enter your *account information*.
- Tap *Next*.

- Tap *Done*.

How To Adjust Display Zoom On iPad

As displays get larger, text is seemingly getting smaller. On certain iOS devices, Apple offers an option to adjust Display Zoom, which not only makes text larger but things like the Home screen icons. Follow along to learn how to enable Display Zoom.

- Open Settings.
- Scroll down to Display & Brightness.
- Under Display Zoom, tap View. You'll now have the option to choose between Standard and Zoomed.

Note that Display Zoom is only available on iPhone 6/7/8 (Plus), iPhone XS Max, iPhone XR, and the third-generation iPad Pro 12.9-inch.

Customize The Dock

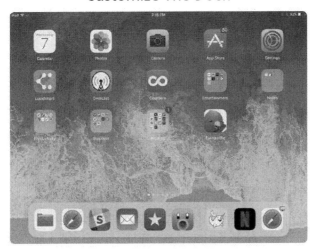

The Dock is your starting point to all interactions on the iPad (along with the Home screen). The Dock is the bottom row of icons which can hold up to 13 apps. And the Dock is available everywhere in iOS. Just a short swipe up from the bottom will take you to the Dock. Then you can just tap on an app to open it.

Fill the Dock with your most used app, and you'll rarely need to go to the Home screen to launch apps.

Swipe Up to Go Home

The new iPads have the same gesture as the iPhone X. Just swipe up to go to the Home screen.

Access App Switcher

A short swipe up will bring up the Dock. And if you swipe up from the bottom of the screen to the middle of the iPad screen, you'll reveal the App Switcher.

Quit Apps

When you're in the App Switcher, just swipe up on an app preview to force quit the app.

Use Apps in Floating Windows

The new iPad Pro comes with iOS 12 and powerful multitasking feature. One really useful feature is Slide Over. When an app is open, just swipe up to open the Dock and drag an app over to the app that's already open. The new app will open in a narrow window. You can move it around and keeping the app that's below it.

Use Split View for Multitasking

The 10.5-inch screen on the iPad Air is great for using two apps side by side (it's going to be a squeeze on the iPad mini). After opening an app, bring up the Dock and drag an app icon from the Dock to either the left or right edge of the screen, till you see a dark box. Release your finger and the app will be docked to the side. You can use the handlebar to resize each app.

Drag and Drop Files or Text Between Apps

Once you have two apps running side by side, you can drag and drop images, text, and files from one app to another.

Watch Videos in Picture in Picture

This feature is enabled by default. When you're watching a video in an app like Netflix, just hit the Home button. The video will continue to play in a small floating window. You can resize it and move it around.

New Way to Access Control Center

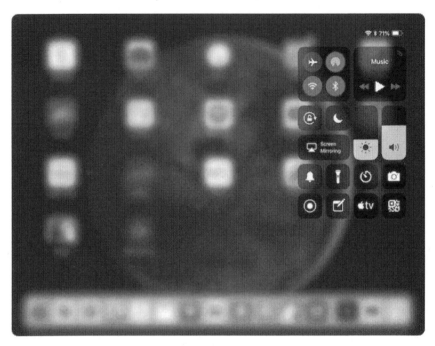

To access Control Center, swipe down from the right edge of the status bar.

Quick Gesture For App Switching

As the iPad Air support iPhone X and iPad Pro gestures, you can quickly switch between apps by using a small arc style gesture. Just swipe left to right, making a small semi-circle, and you'll be able to switch to the most recent app.

Quickly Access Spotlight From Anywhere

There's a huge advantage to using the iPad with a keyboard. Using the Command + Space shortcut, you can bring up Spotlight from anywhere. Start tying an app's name and if it's the first in the suggestions, just press Enter key to open it.

Use Apple Pencil To Take Notes on Lock Screen

The new iPads support the first generation Apple Pencil. Go to Settings -> Notes and you can configure it to automatically launch a new note when you tap the iPad screen with your Apple Pencil on the Lock screen.

Close Multiple Tabs in Safari

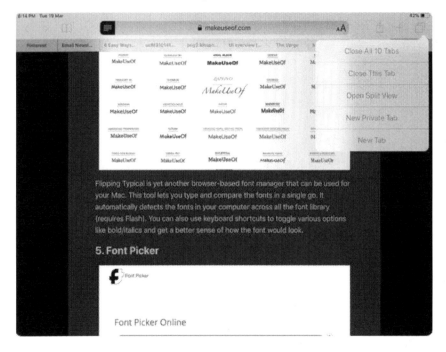

Using Safari on the iPad is an amazing experience. But you do end up opening a lot of tabs quickly. Just tap and hold on the Tab Switcher button and tap on the Close All Tabs button to quickly close all open tabs.

Lock Notes

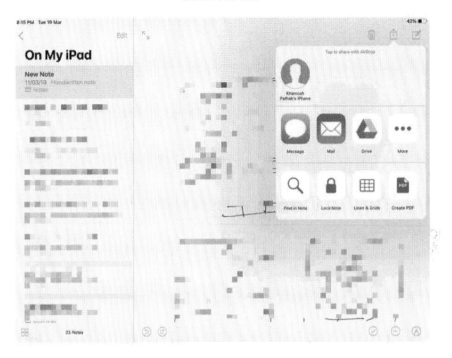

One of the lesser known features of Apple Notes is the ability to lock notes using Touch ID. Open a note, tap on the Share button and select Lock note to get started.

Use Screen Time to Monitor Time Spent

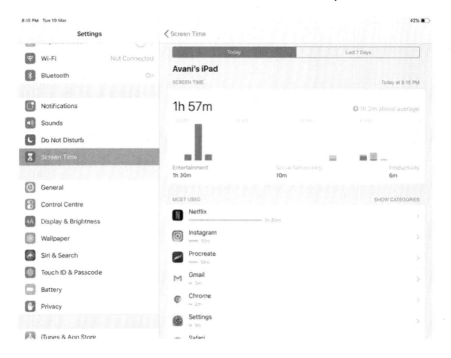

iOS 12 has an awesome new feature called Screen Time that tells you just how much time you're spending on your iPad and it breaks it down based on categories and app usage. Go to Settings -> Screen Time to enable the feature.

Set App Limits

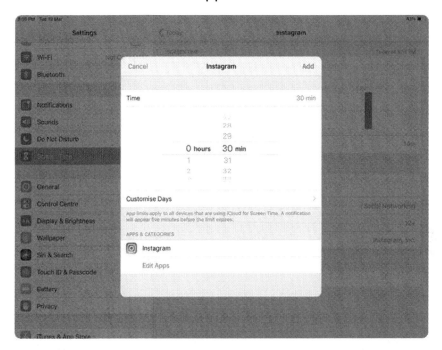

App Limits feature in Screen Time will help you fight your app addiction. If you find yourself spending too much time on Netflix or Facebook, go to Screen Time section, find the app and set an App Limit for it. Set it to be 30 minutes or 1 hour a day.

Move Multiple Apps Together on Home screen

The iPad Pro's home screen is very basic, but at least Apple has made it easier to move things around. You can tap and hold an app icon to put it in wiggle mode. Then drag one icon, so it's out of the grid. Now, with your other hand or finger, you can tap on more apps to add them to the pile of selected icons. Now, move the finger to another page or folder and release it to move all the selected app icons to the next place.

Use The Hidden Cursor Mode

When you have the software keyboard up, just tap and hold on the Space bar to turn the keyboard into a trackpad. Then you can swipe left, right, up or down to move the cursor in those directions. This gives you precise control over the cursor placement.

Enable AssistiveTouch

AssistiveTouch, which gives users a software home button is also available on the iPad. Go to

Settings -> General -> Accessibility -> AssistiveTouch to enable it. Once enabled, you can define double tap and tap and hold gestures for quick actions. The AssistiveTouch button expands when you tap it. You can configure 6 or more actions here as well.

Add Website To Home Screen

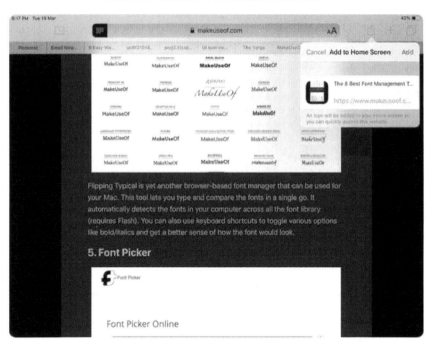

Some things still work better in Safari and negate the need to install a special app. In such a case, you can add websites as Home screen shortcuts. Open the website, tap on Share button and select Add to Home screen.

Use Shortcuts App For Automation

The A12 Bionic chip in the new iPad Air and iPad mini 5 is a beast. There's no app on the App Store that will slow it down. But it still might not be a Laptop replacement because of the software.

The new Shortcuts app by Apple helps bridge some of the gaps. You can create automation workflows that will help you do things that apps on the App Store just can't.

Record Your iPad Screen

You can easily record your iPad screen to show a process to someone. Go to Settings -> Control Center -> Customize Controls and turn on the Screen Recording toggle. Now, open the Control Center and tap Screen Recording toggle to start recording the screen (and the audio if you want).

How to Take a Screenshot

Use the Power and Home button at the same time to take a screenshot. Once a screenshot is taken, you'll see a preview of it in the bottom-left corner. You can tap on it to quickly edit it or share it.

Add Multiple Fingers to Touch ID

When you set up the iPad, you'll only have to add one finger to Touch ID. But you can go to Settings -> Touch ID to add more fingers. You can name individual fingers as well, making it easy to identify if you're sharing the iPad with multiple people.

Use The Smart Keyboard and Master The Keyboard Shortcuts

The iPad is easier to use with keyboard shortcuts, especially if you're dealing with a lot of text. Take a look at some of the shortcuts below. For more information, take a look at our complete iPad keyboard shortcuts guide.

- Command + Left: Go to the end of the line
- Command + Right: Go to the beginning of the current line
- Command + Up: Go to the top of the page
- Command + Down: Go to the bottom of the page
- Option + Left/Right: Move cursor one character at a time
- Option + Shift + Left/Right: Select previous/next word
- Shift + Left/Right: Begin text selection on the Left/Right of the cursor, one character at a time
- Shift + Command + Left/Right: Select the entire line, Left/Right of the cursor
- Shift + Command + Up/Down: Select all text in the document (above or below from the cursor)

Turn off keyboard clicks

The nasty keyboard click of iOS devices is one of the most annoying things you'll hear on public transport. Don't become part of the problem. As standard iOS devices are set to emit a clacky tap sound every time you hit a key no the virtual keyboard. To turn it off go to Settings > Sounds. You'll find the Keyboard Clicks slider right down at the bottom of the list there.

The Quickload bar

One of the Home screen's most important features is the quick-load bar – the dock of icons at the bottom of the screen. You can change what apps feature very easily. Hold down a finger on an app icon until it starts to jiggle. Then drag the app you want on the dock down to it. You can remove dock apps in the same way. Up to six apps can be stored in the quick-load dock.

The notifications bar – how to use it

In iOS 5, released in 2011, Apple introduced an Android-like notifications bar. This is a quick-look update bar that you drag down from the top of the iPad mini's screen. It will show you any recent updates – new messages, new emails, new app alerts and so on. More recently, this notifications bar was updated to let you post, to let you Tweet directly from it – assuming you're logged into Twitter within your iPad mini.

Dictation keyboard

If you're tired of tapping away at the iPad mini's virtual keyboard, you can also talk to it. When connected to a Wi-Fi network, a microphone button will appear on the bottom line of the virtual keyboard. Tap this, and you can freely talk to the iPad. The file will then be piped over to Apple's servers and translated – Siri-style.

How to change wallpapers

You've been able to choose your wallpaper within iOS for some time now, and it's the best way to put your stamp on your iPad mini. To change the wallpaper go to Settings > Brightness & Wallpaper and tap the images of your current wallpaper. You'll then be able to choose your image from the image gallery.

Wallpaper tips

For a perfect iPad mini wallpaper, your source image should be 1,024 x 768 pixels, the same resolution as the tablet's screen. To keep your home screen's icons looking vibrant, you may also want to darken or lighten the wallpaper image so that your tablet's Home screen doesn't look too busy. For Photoshop buffs, we recommend applying a black/white translucent layer of 10-30 percent opacity over the image.

To get the image onto your iPad, sync it using iTunes.

Turn off Push/fetch email

One of the worst offenders of trying to access the web when you're not surfing is email. Getting quick email notifications is great, but it uses up battery. There are two ways to get your email updates, fetch and push. Push automatically sends the data from the server to your iPad mini as soon as it arrived for "instant" updates. Fetch makes the iPad look for the data every so many minute. You can choose from every 15, 30 or 60 minutes, or choose to only look for data manually. You can take your pick in Settings > Mail, Contacts, Calendars.

Switch off location services

Everyone knowing your location is one of the most legitimate "paranoid" concerns of the modern tech age. Plenty of iPad mini apps pinpoint you to a location, and will even make this public knowledge at times. You can turn this feature off if you're worried, within Settings > Privacy. You'll see the Location Services options at the top of this sub-menu.

Check out the Privacy menu to keep control

The iOS 6 software at the heart of the iPad mini keeps track of all the apps that ask for data from other apps – most often things like your calendar or your Twitter account. You can see which apps are trying to access this data in Settings > Privacy. Unless you're downloading some seriously low-rent apps, you shouldn't find anything to worry about, though.

Alerts and notifications

If you find that your iPad mini is bothering you a bit too much, you can turn off notifications for certain apps. This will come in particularly handy if you play free-to-play games – which are generally incessant naggers. Each of your apps gets an entry in the Settings > Notifications menu. You can select whether updates show up, how they appear and whether they pop-up on your lock screen or not.

Do Not Disturb

For an even more carefree life, there's Do Not Disturb. This is a mode that stops all notifications. It's perfect if you fancy an afternoon snooze and don't want to be awoken by the bleat of an attention-seeking iPad mini. The Do Not Disturb mode slider can be found towards the top of the Settings menu.

How to Disable Apple Music Listening History On iPhone And iPad

One of the primary benefits to disabling this feature, especially on iPad, is if you share your iPad between multiple users. This way, Apple Music suggestions don't get confused or jumbled up due to multiple users requesting music at the same time. Learn how to disable this feature.

- Open the Settings app.

- Scroll down until you see Music and tap on it.
- Scroll down until you see Use Listening History.
- Switch the toggle off.

Now, when you play music through the HomePod; it will no longer use it against your listening history, giving you a better overall experience until Apple adds voice profiles.

Transfer Your Cellular Data Plan From Your Old iPad To Your New iPad

If you're picking up a new Cellular iPad to replace a current one, you have some options for transferring over your plan, depending on what kind of SIM card your iPad uses. But whether it's an embedded SIM or nano-SIM, Apple tries to make the process as painless as possible. Follow these steps to learn how to go about moving your iPad cellular data plan over to your new cellular iPad.

- Open Settings on your new iPad Pro.
- Tap Cellular Data.
- Tap Set up Cellular Data.
- Tap the Transfer button if it is available.

If the transfer button doesn't appear in the Setup Cellular Data page, you might need to contact your carrier.

How to play your video files

Getting a video library to play on the iPad mini can be tricky. Like any iOS device, it's tied to iTunes and offers limited codec support. If your videos aren't in MP4 or H.264 formats, they most likely won't play. Already have these formats? No problem. Just add them to your iTunes library on your computer and select them to sync within the iPad mini page that pops-up when you connect.

If you use different formats, such as MKV, you need to do a bit more work. Option one is to transcode your videos using a piece of software like Handbrake – convert them to one to MP4 or H.264 and transfer them as above. Alternatively, you can use a third-party media player app like CineXPlayer HD or MediaPlayer HD Pro. These can play most formats without any conversion. To transfer files, you have to add them as "documents" associated with the app within iTunes.

Set a volume limit (good for kids)

If your iPad mini is going to be used by young folk, it's a good idea to set a music volume limit on it to avoid damage to their hearing. The iPad mini doesn't go loud, but better safe than sorry, eh? To set the limit, go to the Settings menu and scroll down to Music – which has an orange icon. Volume limit is the third item down this sub-menu.

iTunes Match

iTunes Match is Apple's alternative to Spotify – after a fashion. For £21.99 a year, you can stream your music collection without having it stored locally. Up to 25,000 songs can be added. You may end up streaming it at a higher quality than you own too. iTunes Match streams directly from the iTunes library at 256kbps AAC. Up to 10 devices can use iTunes Match, making it a bit of a bargain if you have an iPad, iPhone, Macbook and Apple TV box. To use Match, you need to sign up using iTunes, then flick the iTunes Match switch that you'll find in Settings > iTunes Match on your iPad mini.

How to play FLAC files on an iPad mini

As we found with video, the iPad mini can't play a great variety of files on its own. Apple offers its lossless format, Apple lossless, but audio fans who have a big collection of FLAC or OGG music may not be satisfied with this. Several apps play FLAC and other audiophile files without conversion, including the FLAC player, Golden Ear, and the OPlayer HD. To transfer the files, you have to add them as app documents within iTunes.

iTunes U

One of the more recent additions to the iTunes family is iTunes U. It's a repository of free educational books, video and audio content from the world's educational establishments. You can subscribe for free to these institutions' feeds, making it much like subscribing to a podcast or a digital newspaper. iTunes U has its app too. It's the one with the mortarboard on it. Accessories etc.

How to use AirPrint

AirPrint is built into the iPad mini and lets you print directly from many apps over your Wi-Fi network. It's easy to use, as long as your setup meets a few basic criteria. First, your printer needs to be Wi-Fi enabled. Both your iPad mini and printer need to be connected to the same wireless network for AirPrint to function. Your printer also needs to support AirPrint. Search your printer maker's website to check it is, and always make sure it's running the latest firmware if you encounter problems.

Apple Pay

Apple Pay, which lives inside the Wallet app, keeps all your credit cards, debit cards, store cards, and loyalty cards safe and secure on your iPhone or iPad. With Apple Pay you can use your Visa, Mastercard, American Express card, or Discover Card at any store that accepts tap-to-pay, or in any app that incorporates it. With Wallet, you can also board a plane, scan for your coffee, get into a movie or concert, accumulate loyalty points, and more. All right from your lock screen or with the tap of an icon.

How to Manage Apple Pay

Buying with Apple Pay is incredibly convenient, but it's even more convenient if things like your shipping address are properly set up and ready for you in advance. Once you've made the purchase, being able to see your transactions, both recent and detailed, means never having to wonder about a purchase or wait for a statement again.

How to Use Wallet

Wallet— formerly known as Passbook — is Apple's digital answer to manage the cards that are overfilling your purse, wallet, and pockets. Location aware, Wallet can conveniently present appropriate cards for you right on the lock screen whenever you get close to your coffee shop or airport. Always connected, Wallet can even update your balance or gate number in real time, so you always know how much you have or where you need to be.

How To Set up 'Hey Siri' on iPad

When you set up a new iPhone or iPad, you'll be asked if you want to use "Hey Siri!" voice activation. If you do, you'll be walked through the setup. If you don't, you can change your mind and turn it on at any time in Settings. Here's how!

- Launch **Settings** from your Home screen.
- Tap on **Siri & Search**
- Tap the **Listen for "Hey Siri** switch to turn it on.

How to Train "Hey Siri" to Your Voice

Whether part of the set up process or later, as soon as you turn on "Hey Siri," you'll need to train it to recognize your voice.

- Tap **Set Up Now**.
- Say **Hey Siri!** When prompted.
- Say, **Hey Siri!** Again when prompted.
- Say *Hey Siri!* One more time when prompted.
- Say *Hey Siri, how's the weather?* When prompted.

- Say *Hey Siri; it's me!* When prompted.
- Tap **Done**.

Now, "Hey Siri" will activate — but only if it sounds like your voice.

How to Use "Hey Siri!"

"Hey Siri!" is, by design, ridiculously easy to use. You just say, "Hey Siri" to initiate the start of your interaction.

- Position yourself within audio range of your iPhone or iPad
- Say "Hey Siri!" loud enough for your iPhone or iPad to hear you.
- Tell Siri what you want it to do — "call mom on speaker," "make a dinner reservation," "what's the weather like in Bermuda?", etc.

How Secure Is "Hey Siri!" Voice ID?

We've tested "Hey Siri!" with over a half-dozen voices and nothing has worked except the registered voice or a recording of the registered voice, but that can vary. But Voice ID on Hey Siri isn't meant for security. Don't mistake it for "My voice is my passport, authorize me!" It's meant to solve the problem of unintentional activation, be it accidental, prank, or malicious.

If you're worried about security, turn "Hey Siri" off and stick with manual activation. If you're interested in the convenience of voice activation while you're caring for children, cooking, working, or otherwise have your hands full, then know the limitations but enjoy the functionality.

How to use iCloud

iCloud is Apple's Cloud storage solution. If enabled, it'll backup all sorts of info to Apple's servers. It's so important; it gets its sub-menu within Settings. There you'll find an on-off flick switch for all the information types you can sync, including calendar, mail, contacts, reminders, and photos. To see how much data you're using, tap the Storage & Backup button at the bottom of this sub-menu.

Photostream

One of the most obvious uses for Apple iCloud is Photostream. This uploads all your iPad mini photos to Apple's servers for safekeeping. It'll only do so over Wi-Fi to save you data (if you use a 3G iPad mini). These photos can then be accessed from any other recent iOS devices – iPhones and iPod touches.

iTunes Wi-Fi sync

Although your iPad mini is tied to iTunes, you no longer need to physically connect the tablet to your computer in order to sync. As long as your Mac/PC are on the same Wi-Fi network, you can do so wirelessly. To enable Wi-Fi sync, go to the General tab in your iPad mini's Settings menu while the two devices are hooked-up to the same network.

Switch search engines

Had enough of Google? Your iPad mini can use a couple of other browsers to search the web too. The Safari browser can be set to use Google, Yahoo! or Microsoft's engine Bing. To make your selection go to Settings > Safari. The menu item is at the top of the list.

Private browsing

Safari also offers a private browsing mode, which makes sure not to save any of your histories, or any cookies and so on while you're using the mode. Once again, you'll find this within the Safari sub-menu of the Settings menu.

Adding a second email account

Apple likes to keep things simple, but sometimes this backfires. Try and add a second email account to your iPad mini and you may find you can't. That's because the option isn't within the email client itself but – you guessed it – the entirely separate Settings menu. Go to Settings > Mail, Contacts, Calendars, and at the top of the sub-menu, you'll find the Accounts options. This lists all your current email accounts. At the bottom is an Add Account option.

FaceTime – a primer

FaceTime has been around since 2010. It's an Apple alternative to Skype, letting you video chat for free with other iOS device owners. You can now also chat over 3G. Previously the service was only available over Wi-Fi. FaceTime has its own

iMessage lets you text iPhones

The iPad mini is not a phone, but you can "text" iPhones with one. Its Messaging app uses iMessage. When iPhones are connected to the web, this is what they use to communicate with other iOS devices instead of SMS. You won't receive any of these messages when you're not connected to the net, but it's a super-handy feature.

Check out Whatsapp for other devices

There are ways to contact people not using iOS devices similarly, but you won't get them from Apple. By far the most popular communicator app like this is WhatsApp. It'll let you talk to iPhone owners, Android fans... and even the BlackBerry, Symbian and Windows Phone underclasses. Unfortunately, Whatsapp only works with jailbroken iPads – it's designed for use with phones, and needs to be validated with a phone number.

Download Appshopper for the latest freebies

One of the best app-finding resources for the iPad mini is AppShopper. It's a website, and it's also an app, available for free from iTunes. It's a supremely useful app for gaming and app obsessives, letting you track the latest apps that people are downloading (rather than having to sift through the stream of rubbish releases), and shows you the latest price drops and apps that have recently become freebies.

Download Google Maps, stat

One of the worst parts of the iPad mini's iOS 6 software is something that was meant to be a key feature – Apple Maps. This replaced Google Maps, but poor maps and journey planning earned Apple a bucketful of scorn. For a while, we had to make do, but now Google Maps is available as a separate download from iTunes. It is much, much better. So if you have any need to maps, get download it now.

How to delete apps

Deleting apps on the iPad mini is dead simple. You can do it directly from the home screen. Just hold a finger down an app icon until the icons on-screen start jiggling. Tap the cross on an app's icon no, and you'll be asked if you want to delete it. Simple! Any downloaded apps can easily be re-downloaded from iTunes, by heading into the App Store app, tap Updates and then Purchased. Here you'll find a list of your previously-downloaded apps.

Inverted colors

You can invert the colors of the iPad mini's display – make white black and orange blue. We find it most useful as a prank to play on friends, but it's listed within the accessibility features of the tablet. It may come in handy for colorblind folk, and also cuts down on screen glare if you're reading web pages or books in the dark. To check out the mode go to Settings > General > Accessibility and tap Invert Colors.

"Zoom" mode

If your close-range sight isn't so good, you may appreciate the zoom mode. Tap quickly three times on the Home button and the screen will zoom in by about 30 percent, making everything that bit bigger. It's just for a quick closer look, as it makes part of the screen inaccessible, and does simply stretch the image.

VoiceOver, large text for those with poor sight

There's another accessibility feature that completely changed the way your iPad mini works. It's called VoiceOver and uses voice synthesis to read out the name of anything you put your finger on. Names of apps, text – just about everything. To select an item you tap twice rather than once in this mode. Other accessibility options include being able to ramp-up text size and interface with external Braille accessories (over Bluetooth). To find these options, head to Settings > General > Accessibility.

Move multiple apps at once

Add multiple icons to your selection to move them simultaneously

Like on iPhone, enter the icon jiggle mode then move the first icon slightly so that the "x" disappears. With your other finger, tap all the other icons you'd like to add to your set. You can now bulk-move the icons to a new position by sliding your finger across the screen. Add multiple icons to your selection to move them simultaneously.

Select multiple items

Similar to moving multiple apps on the Home screen at once, you can make a multi-item selection in apps. For instance, in the Files app, you can select multiple files, images, documents, and other items to perform common file operations in bulk.

iOS 12 lets you select multiple items in apps with ease

Just tap and hold the first item until it pops out a bit, then tap other items to add them to the selection while continuing to hold the first item. Plus, you can even use multiple fingers for multitasking and dragging and dropping things across multiple apps.

Split View in Safari

Hold a link and drag it to either side of the screen to open it in Split View side-by-side mode. Alternatively, tap and hold a link and choose Open in Split View from the popup menu.

Split View in Safari is available in landscape on iPad only

If you have a wireless keyboard, press Command-N to open a second tab in Split View. And to open an underlying link on the other side of Split View, simply tap it with three fingers.

Make the screen even dimmer

You can dim the screen brightness below the normal threshold with a low-light filter in conjunction with the zoom feature. Alternatively, go to Settings → General → Accessibility and enable Reduce White Point, then move the slider to the left to reduce the intensity of bright colors.

Position the cursor with precision

You'd be surprised how many people, and even journalists who review technology for a living, are unaware that you can turn the stock iOS keyboard into a virtual trackpad: just rest two fingers anywhere on the keyboard, then slide them across the keyboard.

Hold two fingers on the keyboard for trackpad-like mode

This also works on the iPhone without 3D Touch (tap and hold the Space bar key). If your device has 3D Touch, feel free to take advantage of additional text selection features as well.

Type faster with Key Flicks

Go to Settings → General → Keyboard and slide the switch labeled Enable Key Flicks to the ON position. Now when you use Apple's QuickType keyboard, just flick down on letter keys to enter numbers, symbols and punctuation marks on your iPad.

Swipe down to enter the character from the top of the key

Share charging adapters

Use your USB-C adapters between devices to increase charging speed. For example, your 2018 iPad Pro came with an 18-watt USB-C power adapter that chargers it at the normal rate, but the one that came with your Mac notebook will charge it faster.

You need at least 15/18W USB-C adapter to fast-charge your iPhone/iPad

With a Lighting to USB-C cable, your iPad Pro adapter can even fast-charge your iPhone and previous iPad Pros. Apple also sells this charger separately as an option for iPhone owners who would like to take advantage of the fast-charge capability.

Restart without the Home button

To restart your iPad faster, go to Settings → General → Accessibility → Assistive Touch, then turn it on and tap Customize Top Level Menu to add a Restart action.

AssistiveTouch can be quite handy, especially if the Home button is broken

You can now bring up the AssistiveTouch overlay at any time by triple-pressing the Power or Side button. AssistiveTouch is an especially useful Home button software replacement for older iPhones and iPads that have a broken Home button.

How to Crop or Zoom a Video on iMovie for iOS

Want to crop a video or movie in iMovie on the iPhone or iPad? Cropping a video in iMovie allows you to essentially zoom in on a movie, either to crop out unnecessary elements, to reframe the video to emphasize something else, or to zoom into what you'd rather the video highlight. Cropping is different from trimming a video which is used to shorten the total length to cut out extraneous content.

iMovie for iOS allows you to crop videos, but it's not particularly obvious, as there is no crop button, and instead, the iMovie for iOS app indirectly refers to the crop capability by calling it to zoom. And like many other features of iOS, the function to crop video in iMovie on the iPhone or iPad is hidden behind a few layers of interface abstraction that can be easily overlooked, or remain totally unknown to many using iMovie, leading many iPhone and iPad users to believe that there is no crop functionality in iMovie for iOS. But not to worry, you can crop a video in iMovie directly on your iPhone or iPad, and you won't need to download any third party apps to do so.

How to Crop / Zoom a Video in iMovie for iPhone or iPad

This works to crop/zoom any movie you can import into iMovie on iOS. The screenshots here demonstrate this on an iPhone with iMovie rotated sideways into landscape mode, but aside from the appearance, it's the same in landscape or iPad too.

Before getting started, be sure you have iMovie installed on your iPhone or iPad, and that the video or movie you want to crop/zoom is on the device itself.

- Open iMovie in iOS if you have not done so already, then tap on the "Projects" and click the big plus sign "+ Create Project" button

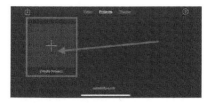

○ Select "Movie" from the options

- Select the video you want to crop from your iOS library so that it has a little blue check mark on it, then tap on the text "Create Movie" button

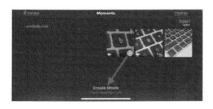

○ iMovie will open the video into the project, now tap on the video timeline / scrubber section

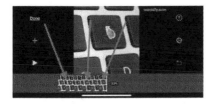

- An additional toolbar will be revealed, along with a tiny magnifying glass in the corner of the video, tap on that tiny grey magnifying glass in the corner to enable the crop/zoom feature of iMovie in iOS

  ○ When the magnifying glass says "Pinch to zoom video" you can now use a pinch or spread gesture on the movie preview to zoom and crop the video, do that until the video is cropped / zoomed sufficiently to your needs

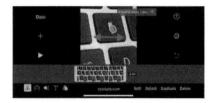

- When satisfied with your cropped/zoomed video, tap the grey "Done" text button

- Now you can save and export the freshly cropped movie from iMovie and save the video to the iPhone or iPad camera roll, so tap on the Sharing / Action button that looks like a box with an arrow flying out of the top

- Select where you want to save the video, or how you want to share it, in the example here we are choosing "Save Video" which saves the cropped movie to the iOS Camera Roll in Photos app (yes your videos in iOS will be stored in the Photos app)

○ Choose the size you want to export the video, remember HD video sizes are larger but higher quality compared to the other video exporting settings

Now you can return to the Photos app and go to your Camera Roll or to the Videos folder of Photos to find the freshly cropped/zoomed video you just saved and exported

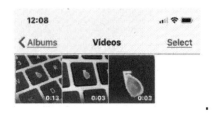

The cropped or Zoom a Video saved from iMovie into the Videos section of the Photos app

It's noteworthy that when you're saving the video initially, the thumbnail may not show the cropped/zoomed video, but despite not showing that the video has been cropped or zoomed in that thumbnail when you look at the actual saved and exported video, it will be cropped. You can see this in the example screenshots of the video cropped in this tutorial, which shows a worn out "E" key on a Mac laptop.

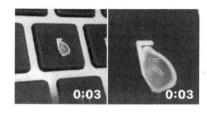

Example of a cropped zoomed video from iMovie for iOS

It's also important to point out that cropping or zooming a video will result in some loss of quality, with more loss of quality happening the greater the zoom or crop because you are essentially shrinking down the available pixels used in the video to highlight them.

Being able to crop and zoom a video is useful for many reasons, particularly if you recorded a movie on the iPhone or iPad but find that it's not particularly focused on a subject, or if you decide you'd like to change the focus of the video itself. Another useful feature is trimming a video in iOS which you can do directly in the video viewer of Photos app, or by using the same general principals in the iMovie for iOS app.

If you're an Apple user with a variety of devices, you may already know how to crop a video in iMovie for Mac, which is a bit more intuitive thanks to the obvious crop button. Alas, iMovie for iOS has no such obvious Crop button and instead hides it as a "Zoom" feature that is quite subtle without it being pointed out to the user or explained, as we do in this tutorial. So if you have hunted around in iMovie for iPhone or iPad for a cropping feature and not found one, don't feel bad, it's really quite hidden, much like the ability to rotate a video in iMovie on iPhone or iPad is hidden as basically an invisible gesture within the app. Perhaps a future version of iMovie for iOS will make a more obvious Crop

Video feature available in iMovie or even in the default Video viewer of Photos app (like the crop photos feature of iOS that already exists), but until or if that ever happens, you can remember to use the Zoom button and pinch gestures to crop a video in iMovie for iOS instead.

Tap the Title Bar

Have you ever scrolled down a long list or been at the bottom of a large web page and needed to get back to the top? There's no need to scroll. Most of the time, you can tap the title bar of the app or web page to return to the beginning of the list. This works with most apps and most web pages, although not every web page is designed to be iPad-friendly.

Skip the Apostrophe

Skipping the apostrophe is also a great time-saver and ranks as my number one keyboard tip. This secret relies on auto-correct to do some of the typing for us. The auto-correct feature on the iPad can be quite annoying, but at times, it can also save you some time.

The coolest trick is the ability to insert an apostrophe for most contractions like 'can't' and 'won't.' Simply type the words without the apostrophe, and autocorrect will usually insert it for you.

You can also use the predictive typing suggestions that appear at the top of the keyboard to help speed up your typing, and if you don't like the on-screen keyboard, you can install a third-party keyboard from companies like Google or Grammarly.

The Virtual Touchpad

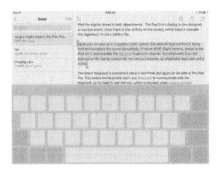

Possibly the number one thing people miss about their PC is the mouse. The ability to tell your computer what to do by touching the screen is great for ordinary uses, but when you want to do a lot of typing, the ability to move the cursor with a touchpad or mouse is... well, there are few substitutes.

This might be why Apple added a virtual touchpad to the iPad's on-screen keyboard. This often overlooked secret can make a world of distance if you frequently create long messages or lists using the iPad. Simply hold two or more fingers down on the on-screen keyboard and move your fingers without lifting them from the display and a cursor within the text will move with your fingers.

Open Apps and Find Music and Quickly Using Spotlight Search

Did you know the iPad has a universal search feature? There's no need to go hunting through pages and pages of apps for just the right one, and no reason to open music just to play a song. Spotlight Search can find anything from music to videos to contacts to apps on your device. It will even suggest websites to visit.

You can launch Spotlight Search by swiping down with your finger while you are on the Home Screen, which is the name of the screen with all of your apps on it. Any time you are on the Home Screen (i.e., not inside an app or using Siri), you can swipe down to initiate a

Spotlight Search. The key here is to swipe down somewhere in the middle of the screen. If you swipe from the very top of the display, you will open the Notification Center.

The great thing about Spotlight Search is that it searches your entire device, so you can even use it to search for a specific text message or email. It will even search through Notes. You can turn on and off different results through the general settings of your iPad under Spotlight Search.

Download Free Books on Your iPad

Everyone likes free stuff! And you can get plenty of freebies with your iPad if you know where to look. For book lovers, the best-kept secret on the iPad comes from something called Project

Gutenberg. The goal of Project Gutenberg is to take the world's library of public domain works and convert them to digital. Treasure Island, Dracula, Alice in Wonderland, and Peter Pan are just a few of the books you can download for free on your iPad.

- If you haven't already done so, you'll first need to download the iBooks application. This is Apple's digital bookstore and reader
- After you launch the iBooks app, tap the Top Charts button at the bottom of the screen. This will bring up two lists: the top Paid books and the top Free books.
- Tap the Categories button at the top-left corner of the screen. This will drop down a categories list. If you are interested in reading some of the greatest literature of all time without paying a dime, select Fiction and Literature from the list.
- You will now be able to scroll through the most popular free novels available through

iBooks. You can further narrow the list by choosing a category like Sci-Fi & Fantasy or Young Adult.

Move an App to the iPad's Dock

Do you hate scrolling through multiple screens of apps looking for your favorite one? There are several tricks for finding an app on your iPad quickly, including using spotlight search, but one of the most overlooked tricks is simply docking your favorite app.

The dock refers to the final row of apps at the very bottom of the iPad's display. These apps are always present on the Home screen, which means you don't have to scroll through page after page of apps to find them. And the best part is that you can move any app you want to the dock.

The iPad comes with five apps on the dock, but the new flexible dock can hold many more apps. The last two spots are reserved for your most recently used apps, which helps when you multitask using the iPad, but the rest of the dock is yours to customize. You can even move a folder full of apps to the dock.

- First, touch the app you want to move and leave your finger on the screen until the app icons are jiggling. This puts the iPad's home screen into edit mode, which lets you either move or delete an app.
- Next, move your finger. The app icon will move with your finger. If you accidentally picked your finger up from the screen, you can still grab the app by tapping on it and moving your finger without lifting it from the screen.

- You can dock an app by moving it to the dock. You will want to place it between two existing apps on the dock and wait until those apps move apart to provide space for the app you want on the dock.

Let Your iPad Read Selected Text to You

Do you want to give your eyes a rest? Let your iPad do the heavy lifting -- or, in this case, the heavy reading — for you. The iPad can speak selected text to you, but first, you will need to turn this feature on in the accessibility settings. The text-to-speech feature is designed to help the visually impaired, but it can be very useful to most people. For example, the iPad could allow you to multitask by reading an interesting news article to you while you cook dinner.

How to Turn On the iPad's Text-to-Speech Feature

- First, go into the iPad's settings.
- Next, choose General settings from the left-side menu.
- Tap Accessibility from within the General settings. It is just above the section for Multitasking Gestures.
- From within the Accessibility settings, choose Speech. This is the last option in the Vision block.
- Turn on Speak Selection by tapping the associated slider. This setting will add a new Speak option to the menu that appears when you select text.
- If you think you may use the feature often, you can also turn on Speak Screen. This allows you to slide two fingers down from the top of the display to read the entire

screen to you. This doesn't work so well with web pages where the top of the screen is filled with menus, but it works well with other apps like Mail.

- You can also change the voice used by tapping the Voices button within the Speech settings. Also, pay attention to the Speaking Rate. This can be adjusted to have the iPad speak faster or slower.

One great way to use the text-to-speech feature is within iBooks, where the iPad can read the book to you. This isn't quite as good as a book on tape, where the reader can give the right inflection to the words and sometimes even portray the character's voices. However, if you choose to speak to the screen, the iPad will automatically turn pages and keep reading the book.

Changes to Notifications in iOS 12

In iOS 12, Apple has introduced new notification features, providing expanded set of tools for monitoring and managing notifications in quicker and more intuitive ways.

There have been no changes to the way that Notifications work on the whole, but many of these features make it easier to clear notifications, determine which notifications you want, and make adjustments on the fly.

Grouped Notifications

iPad owners have been asking for the return of grouped notifications for years, and in iOS 12, Apple delivered. Multiple notifications from the same app will be grouped on the Lock screen of the iPhone, cutting down on clutter. You can tap a set of notifications from a particular app to expand them to see all of the notifications in the list.

You can tap on the "X" next to a notification group to clear all of those notifications at one time, or do the same thing with a swipe to the left.

In the Settings app, you can change the behavior of grouped notifications. Go to Settings > Notifications and tap on any app to see the "Notification Grouping" preferences. Tap that to choose "Automatic," "By App," or "Off" if you'd rather see all of the incoming notifications for a particular app like Messages.

Automatic sorts by the app for the most part, but with this setting enabled, you might get two notification groups if you have email threads going with two different people in the Mail app, or multiple conversations in Messages, for example. Or different incoming Messages conversations. By App will make sure all notifications from an app are in one stack, without the sorting that Automatic mode uses.

Instant Tuning

Instant Tuning is a feature that lets you manage a pesky notification right on the Lock screen, giving you the tools to turn notifications for that app off entirely or send notifications right to the Notification Center.

On any notification that's on the Lock screen or in the Notification Center when you swipe down, swipe left on a notification to see settings that include "Manage," "View," and "Clear All."

Select "Manage" from this list to see Instant Tuning options. Notifications set to "Deliver Quietly" will be visible in Notification Center, but you won't see them on the Lock screen, there will be no banner, and there won't be a badge.

To reverse this, tap on a notification from the muted app again, follow the same instructions, and choose "Deliver Prominently." Notification settings can also be changed in the Settings app, also accessible from the Instant Tuning popup. Turn Off, as the name suggests, turns off notifications for that app entirely.

You can also get to your Instant Tuning settings by 3D Touching or long pressing on any notification and selecting the three ellipses.

Note: In iOS 12, Apple will send you alerts asking you if you would like to continue receiving notifications from a particular app if you've been getting a lot of notifications and haven't been interacting with them. When this happens, the alert will feature a "Manage" section so you can access your Instant Tuning settings for that particular app.

Critical Alerts

Critical Alerts are a new type of opt-in notification in iOS 12 that can ignore your Do Not Disturb settings to send important must-see notifications.

These alerts are limited in scope and are available for medical and health-related information, home security, and public safety.

For example, a person who is diabetic might want to set critical alerts for a glucose monitor when blood sugar is low, so the notification will be delivered even if Do Not Disturb is turned on.

Critical alerts bypass Do Not Disturb and the ringer switch, and will always play a sound. They are meant to be disruptive and for that reason, are going to be highly limited to apps that need these kinds of immediate alerts.

Developers with apps appropriate for critical alerts will need to apply for an entitlement that needs to be approved by Apple. Users will be able to turn off critical alerts on a per-app basis separately from other notifications.

Notification Count in Screen Time

Screen Time, Apple's new feature designed to provide you with the tools to monitor when and how you're using your iOS devices, keeps track of all of the notifications that apps are sending you, letting you know which apps are the noisiest.

This information can help you decide if you want to keep notifications turned on for a particular app, or if you might want to mute an app to cut down on interruptions.

You can get to this section of Screen Time by opening the Settings app, choosing Screen Time, selecting "All Devices," and then scrolling down to the bottom. You can see your notifications from for the last 24 hours or the last seven days.

Richer Notifications

In iOS 12, app developers can build notifications that can accept user input, so you can interact with notifications in new ways, doing more on the Lock screen without having to open up your iPhone.

With Instagram, as an example, if the app sends you a notification that a friend posted, you might be able to view the photo and then add a like all from the notification.

In this example, you can tap the heart to like the photo, something that wasn't possible in iOS 11. Rich notifications were available in earlier versions of iOS, but Apple has removed the limits that previously restricted interactive touches.

How to Hide Pictures From the Photos App in iOS 12

Sometimes you might not want certain pictures shot on your iPhone or iPad to take pride of place in your Photo Library, but for whatever reason, you don't want to just outright delete them. Fortunately, Apple's Photos app includes an option to hide certain photos from the main library. This article shows you how.

Bear in mind that hiding pictures via the following method ensure they won't appear in the Photos or For You sections of the Photos app, but they will still be accessible in the Albums section. If you're looking for a more secure way to squirrel away pictures, consider using a third-party app like Safe Lock instead.

How to Hide Pictures in the Photos App

- Launch the Photos app on your iPhone or iPad.
- Tap Select in the top-right corner of the screen.
- Tap the pictures you want to hide.
- Tap the Share button in the bottom-left corner of the screen. (It looks like a square with an arrow pointing out.)
- In the Share Sheet's bottom row of available actions, tap Hide.
- Tap the prompt that appears at the bottom of the screen to confirm.

Note that pictures you choose to hide from your photo library are stored in an album called Hidden, which lives in the Albums tab.

How to Unhide Pictures in the Photos App

- Launch the Photos app on your iPhone or iPad.
- Tap the Albums tab at the bottom of the screen.
- Scroll to the bottom and under Other Albums, tap Hidden.
- Tap Select in the top-right corner of the screen.
- Tap the pictures you want to unhide.
- Tap the Share button at the bottom-left corner of the screen.
- In the Share Sheet's bottom row of available actions, tap Unhide.

How to Use iCloud Keychain on Your iOS Devices

iCloud Keychain is a feature of your Apple account that you can use to keep your website login credentials, personal details, credit card details, and wireless network information up to date and available across all your Apple devices.

With so many usernames and passwords to remember these days, iCloud Keychain provides a convenient way of always having this information at hand. And with its AutoFill feature, iCloud Keychain can even enter your credentials for you when required.

It's also very secure, thanks to Apple's use of end-to-end encryption. This means that only you can access your information, and only on devices where you're signed in to iCloud.

How to Enable iCloud Keychain on Your iPhone or iPad

- Open the Settings app and tap your Apple ID banner at the top of the Settings menu.
- Tap iCloud.
- Scroll down the list and select Keychain.

- Toggle on the iCloud Keychain switch and enter your Apple ID password if prompted.

If this is the first time you've enabled iCloud Keychain, you'll be asked to create an iCloud Security Code or use your existing device passcode. You'll also need to enter a phone number where you can receive SMS messages for authorization purposes. If you've already enabled iCloud Keychain in the past, you'll be prompted to enter the passcode that was used to set it up previously.

Accessing Your Login Details in iCloud Keychain

With iCloud Keychain enabled, Apple's Autofill feature will fill in your login credentials for you whenever you come across the relevant input fields on a website or in an app. On occasion, you may encounter a login screen that doesn't play nice with Autofill. In such cases, you'll need to copy and paste your username and password manually. Here's how it's done:

- Open the Settings app on your iOS device.
- Tap Accounts and Passwords.
- Tap App & Website Passwords and use Touch ID if prompted.
- Tap the relevant login entry in the list, or using the search field at the top of the Passwords screen, type in the name of the app or website for which you need login credentials.
- Long press on the username/password and tap the Copy pop-up option.
- Now navigate back to the relevant app or website, long press the username/password input field, and then tap the Paste pop-up option.

Note that you can delete login credentials by tapping Edit at the top right of the Passwords screen. You can also tap a website entry and use the Edit option to change existing username and password fields.

Adding Credit Cards and Personal Information

You can add personal information and credit card information to iCloud Keychain at any time using your iPad, after which it will be available across all of your devices. Simply follow these steps:

- Open the Settings app.
- Tap Safari.
- Tap AutoFill.
- To add personal information, tap My Info and select your contact card from the list of contacts. To add credit card details, tap Saved Credit Cards and then tap Add Credit Card.

Troubleshooting common problems

Having issues and problems with your iPad? Don't worry; we will take you on some common problems of iPad and how you can easily fix them.

Why won't my iPad turn on?

1. Turn your iPad off and on

- On an iPad with no Home Button and iPhones X or later: press and hold the Side/Top/Power button and either volume button until the slider appears

- On an iPad or iPhone with a Home Button and iPod Touch: press and hold the

Side/Top/Power button until the slider appears

- Drag the slider to turn the device off and after the device turns off, press and hold that Side/Top/Power button again until you see the Apple Logo

- With iOS 11 and above, restart using
Settings > General > Shut Down

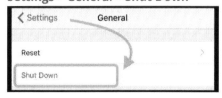

2. *Reset or force restart your iPad*

- On an iPad with no Home Button and iPhones 8 or later: Press and quickly release the Volume Up button. Press and immediately release the Volume Down button. Then press and hold the Side/Top/Power button until the device restarts

- On an iPhone 6s and earlier, iPad with a Home Button, or iPod touch: Press and hold both the Home and the Top (or Side) buttons for at least 10 seconds, until you see the Apple logo

Why is my iPad not responding or slow to respond to my touch?

- It may be that your screen is dirty. Try cleaning your screen
- To do this, unplug everything, turn off iPad (see above), then with a very soft, lint-free

and slightly damp cloth gently wipe the screen. Do NOT use window cleaners and paper towels
- If you have any screen protector sheet, try removing it

Why isn't my iPad showing up in iTunes when connected?

- Check that your Lightning port is clear of any dusty, debris, or dirt
- Make sure that you have the latest version of iTunes
- iPad requires USB 2.0 or higher to function properly. Unplug your iPad from your computer, and plug it into a different USB port
- Turn your iPad off and on
- Disconnect your iPad from your computer, then turn your computer off and on and reconnect
- Especially for Windows users, if the above steps do not resolve your issue, uninstall

iTunes entirely and then reinstall the latest version of iTunes

My WiFi connection doesn't work on my iPad; how do I fix it?

- Turn WiFi off and then on by tapping Settings > Wi-Fi
- Make sure that your Wi-Fi router and the modem is on
- Update your Wi-Fi software to the latest version.
- Turn your iPad off and on by holding the On/Off button until "slide to power off" shows
- Turn your Wi-Fi router off and on
- Change your DNS settings to use Google's Public DNS of 8.8.8.8 and 8.8.4.4.
- Tap Settings > General > Reset > Reset Network Settings and reset your network settings

Why isn't an app or the App Store app working on my iPad?

- Update your iPad to the latest iOS version
- Check to see if there is an update for your app, if there is, update (App Store > Updates)
- Only one app with issues? Try closing the app by double pressing Home or swiping up the Home Gesture Bar and swiping up on the problem app's preview to close it.

Then relaunch that app and see if it works normally

- Turn your iPad off and on
- Force restart your iPad by pressing both the home and power buttons and maintain this hold until you see the Apple logo on the screen. Then release the buttons and the iPad restarts
- Remove the app. You may want to backup before removing any app. Tap and hold on the app icon until the icons start to wiggle.

Just tap the "x" button to delete an app. After removing the app, go to the App Store and reinstall it.

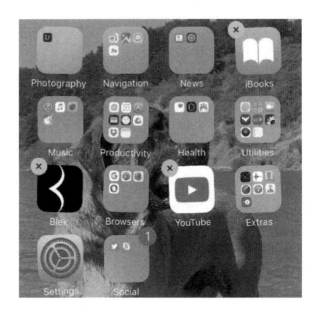

Why is my iPad not charging or is charging very slow?

- To charge your iPad, you can try either connecting your iPad to a power outlet or connecting to a port on your computer using the charging cable that came with your iPad.

- Computers generally don't supply enough power to their USB ports to be able to charge an iPad. When this happens, a "Not Charging" message appears
- Check that your Lightning Port on both your iPad and your charger is clean and clear of any debris, lint, or dust

How do I stop my iPad battery from draining?

- Change your notification settings to Show Previews only when unlocked instead of alway
- Use headphones or earphones instead of your iPad's speakers
- Turn off background app refresh

- Turn down your iPad's screen brightness or have your iOS manage brightness settings via Auto-Brightness

- Set your iPad's Auto-Lock to 30 seconds via Display & Brightness Settings
- Switch off the Data Roaming Setting – Even in older iPads, we have seen that the wi-fi/cellular settings can cause battery

drain. Switching off the Data Roaming may help in addressing this issue.

- If you have the Wi-Fi/Cellular iPad, tap on Settings > Cellular Data > Toggle off. Do the same for the other mobile options, i.e., Cellular Data > Cellular Data Options > Enable LTE to off and Data Roaming to off
- Once you have set the settings to off; next you can toggle them back to ON. This simple toggling of Cellular related options can often fix battery issues on an iPad that has both Wi-Fi and Cellular

Sometimes the iPad consumes excessive battery if there is a process in the stuck mode

Try doing a forced restart on the iPad.

Let the device charge until 100% and then start using it and see if it made a difference to your situation.

My iPad is stuck in a reboot loop! How do I fix my iPad from restarting?

- The chances are that your iPad has insufficient battery power even to start up
- Usually, iPads don't attempt to restart until there is enough battery power.
- But for you (and some unlucky others), something is telling the iPad to try to boot even though the battery can't last long enough to finish.
- Hence, the loop you experience–charging a little, attempting a boot, shutting off, charging a little, trying to boot and so forth again and again.

We need to get your iPad sufficiently charged to complete a normal and full boot cycle

- Plug the iPad into a power source. Ideally, use the charger that came with your iPad. DO NOT plug it into your computer
- Next, hold down the home button and the power button simultaneously for as long as you possibly can–the longer, the better– and ideally at least 30 minutes to 1 hour

- Holding down these two buttons prevents that loop cycle. That allows your iPad to charge up a bit. Think creatively about how to hold these buttons down for a length of time
- As soon as you release these buttons, your iPad tries to boot. If you don't hold Home and Power long enough for a sufficient charge, that loop pattern continues
- So try and hold down these buttons for as long as possible-or create some makeshift tools to assist-keep these gentle, so they don't cause other damage

I believed this quick guide had helped you to master your iPad Air and iPad mini. Thank you for purchasing this book!

Printed in Great Britain
by Amazon